From Seed to Pine Tree

Following the Life Cycle

by
Suzanne Slade

illustrated by
Jeff Yesh

PICTURE WINDOW BOOKS
Minneapolis, Minnesota

Thanks to our advisers for their expertise, research, and advice:

Kathryn Orvis, Ph.D., Associate Professor/Extension Specialist
Department of Youth Development & Agricultural Education
Purdue University, West Lafayette, Indiana

Terry Flaherty, Ph.D., Professor of English
Minnesota State University, Mankato

Editor: Shelly Lyons
Designer: Lori Bye
Page Production: Melissa Kes
Art Director: Nathan Gassman
Editorial Director: Nick Healy
The illustrations in this book were created digitally.

Picture Window Books
151 Good Counsel Drive
P.O. Box 669
Mankato, MN 56002-0669
877-845-8392
www.picturewindowbooks.com

Photo Credits: U.S. Department of Agriculture-Forest Service,
Southern Research Station, 23

Library of Congress Cataloging-in-Publication Data
Slade, Suzanne.
From seed to pine tree : following the life cycle / by Suzanne Slade ;
illustrated by Jeff Yesh.
p. cm. — (Amazing Science: Life Cycle)
Includes index.
ISBN 978-1-4048-5162-7 (library binding)
1. Pine—Life cycles—Juvenile literature. I. Yesh, Jeff, 1971- ill. II. Title.
QK494.5.P66S53 2009
585'.2—dc22   2008037904

Table of Contents

Beautiful Pines

Pine trees are known for their long, thin leaves called needles. Pine trees are evergreens, so their needles stay green year-round. These beautiful trees are found in forests, parks, and maybe even your yard. More than 150 different kinds of trees belong to the pine family. They all have the same basic life cycle. Let's look at the life cycle of the shortleaf pine tree.

STATE PARK

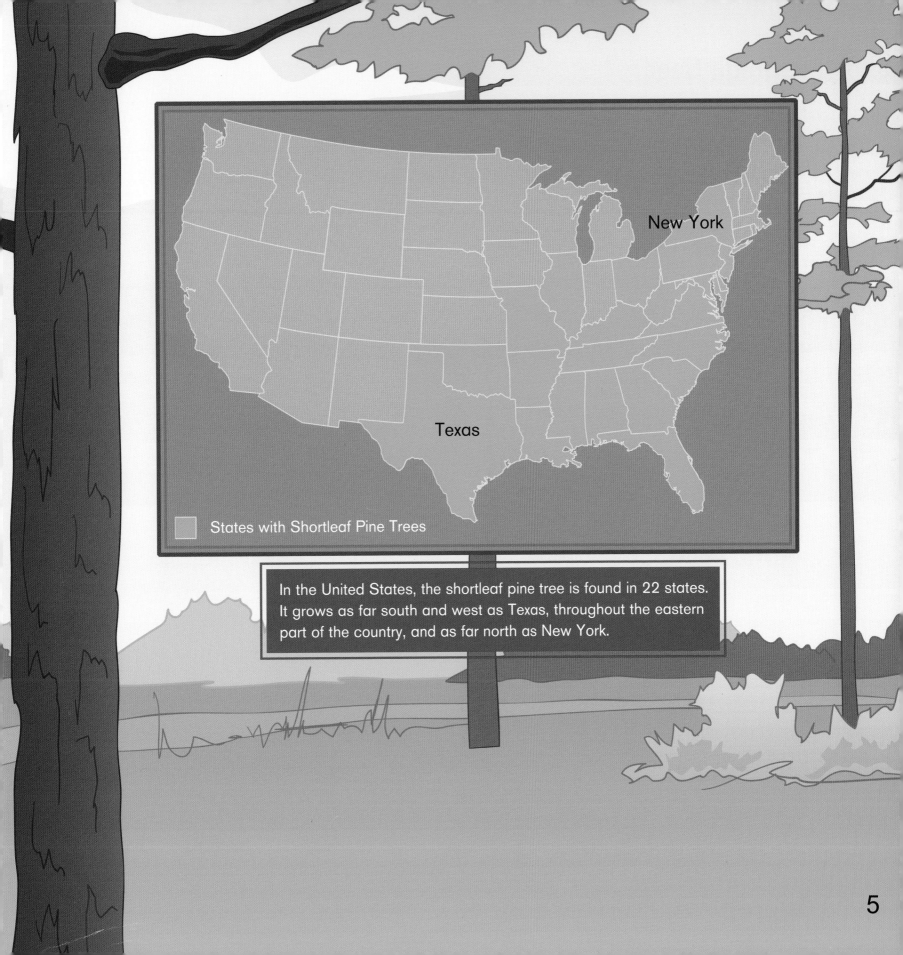

New York

Texas

States with Shortleaf Pine Trees

In the United States, the shortleaf pine tree is found in 22 states. It grows as far south and west as Texas, throughout the eastern part of the country, and as far north as New York.

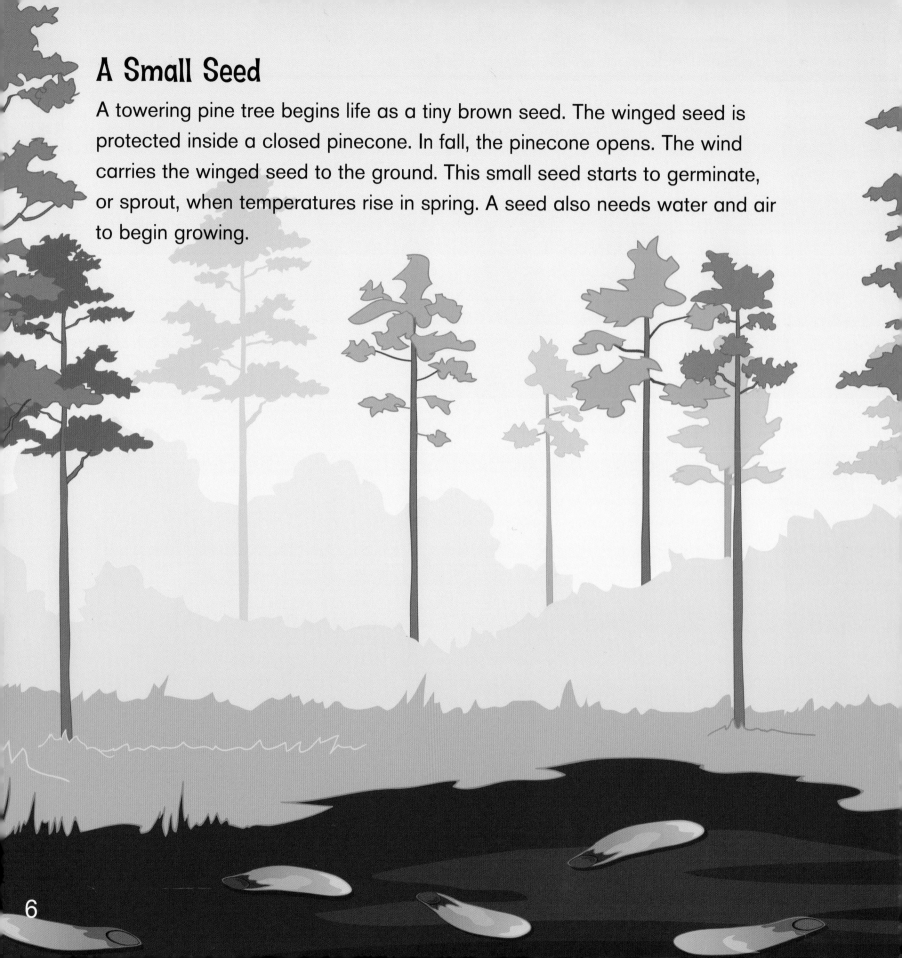

A Small Seed

A towering pine tree begins life as a tiny brown seed. The winged seed is protected inside a closed pinecone. In fall, the pinecone opens. The wind carries the winged seed to the ground. This small seed starts to germinate, or sprout, when temperatures rise in spring. A seed also needs water and air to begin growing.

A seed has nutrients, or food, inside itself to help it grow.
It uses this food until the plant is big enough to make its own.

A Seedling Sprouts

When a seed begins to sprout, the tough outer coat of a seed opens. Soon, tiny roots grow downward into the ground. They take in water and hold the seed in place. Soon, a green shoot sprouts upward toward the bright sunlight. Next, green needles grow from the shoot. The seed has become a young tree called a seedling.

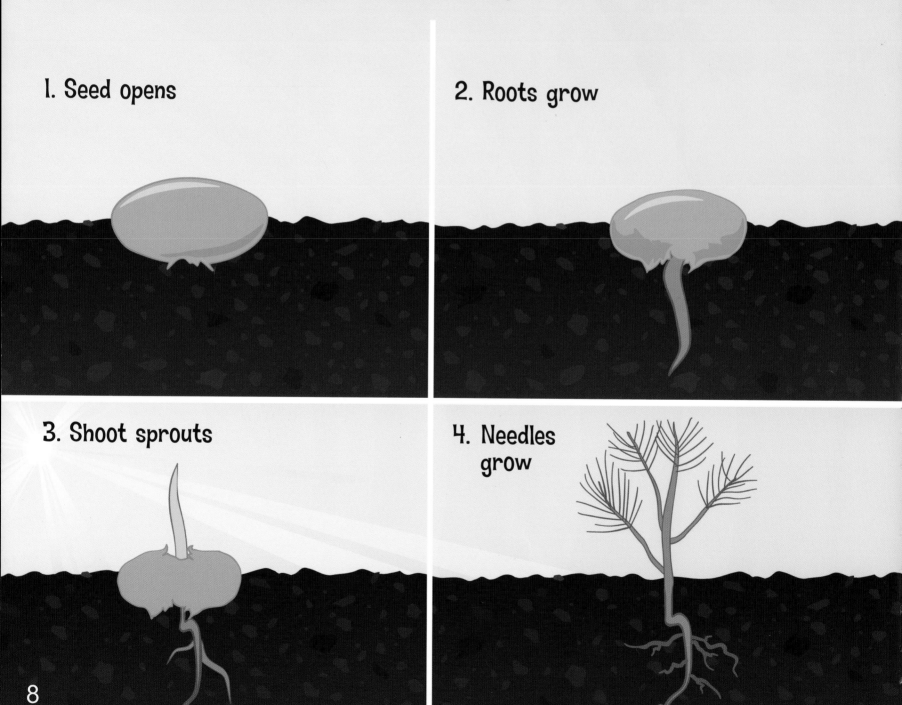

1. Seed opens

2. Roots grow

3. Shoot sprouts

4. Needles grow

seedling

Most shortleaf pine seedlings die before they are a year old. Sometimes this happens because seedlings do not get enough water. Other seedlings are eaten by hungry insects. Often, too many seeds fall in a small area. There may not be enough nutrients for all of them to survive.

Growing Tall

A seedling needs air, sunlight, and water to grow. It uses these things to make food in its needles. This process is called photosynthesis. A shortleaf pine seedling becomes a sapling when it is 3 years old. A sapling has a strong, woody trunk and looks like its parent tree.

oxygen

During photosynthesis, pine trees make a gas called oxygen in their long needles. People and animals need oxygen to live.

A Mighty Pine

A sapling grows taller each year, until it becomes a mighty pine tree. When a shortleaf pine tree is 20 years old, it will be about 60 feet (18 meters) tall. Most full-grown shortleaf pine trees reach a height of 100 feet (31 m). That's about as tall as a 10-story building!

In fall, some of the shortleaf pine tree's needles turn brown and fall off. Other needles stay green all winter. That's why it is called an evergreen tree. In spring, a pine tree grows new needles on the tips of its branches.

10 stories

13

Flowers Called Pinecones

When a shortleaf pine tree is 20 years old, it grows special flowers in the spring. The flowers are called pinecones. Some pinecones are male, and others are female. New male pinecones are smaller than female pinecones. The long, thin male pinecones are yellow or green. New female pinecones are green.

new male
pinecones

new female
pinecones

The thick scales on the female pinecones later turn brown and hard. The male pinecones also turn brown as time goes on.

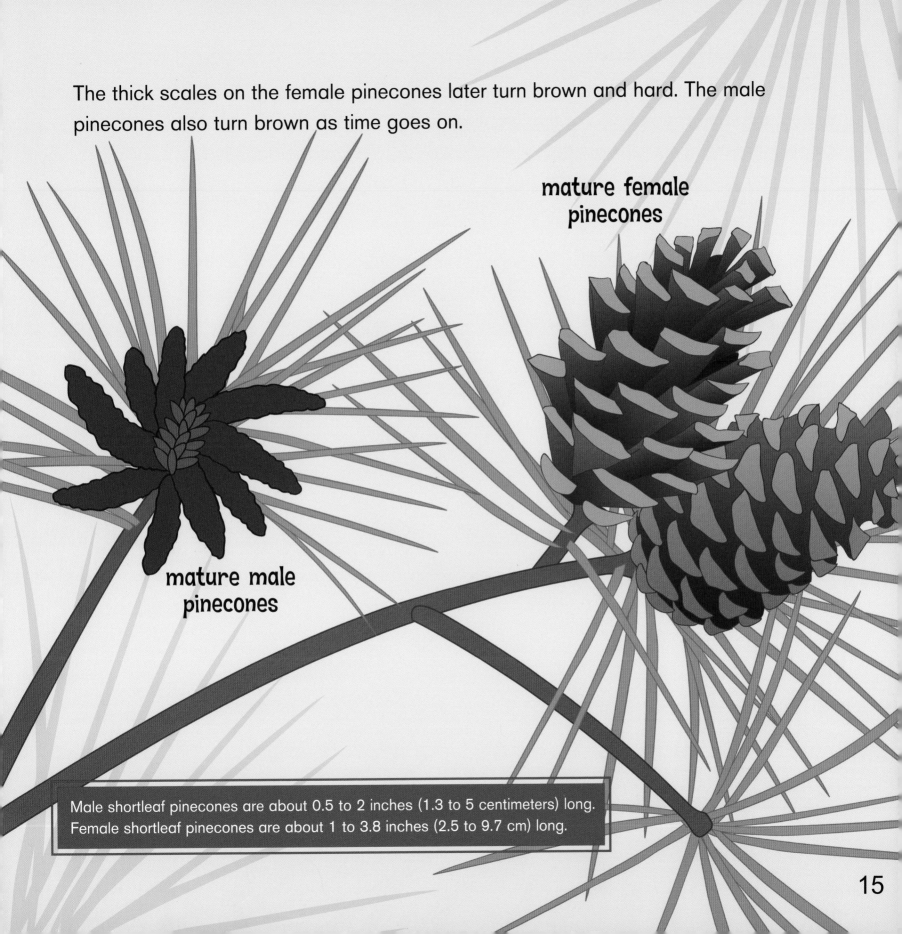

mature female
pinecones

mature male
pinecones

Male shortleaf pinecones are about 0.5 to 2 inches (1.3 to 5 centimeters) long.
Female shortleaf pinecones are about 1 to 3.8 inches (2.5 to 9.7 cm) long.

Making New Seeds

Male pinecones make a yellow dust called pollen. The wind blows some of this pollen onto the open scales of the female pinecones. Soon, the female scales close, trapping the pollen inside. When the pollen fertilizes the eggs inside of a female pinecone, new pine tree seeds start to form.

16

Female pinecones can be fertilized by male pinecones on the same tree.

Flying Free

When the new seeds are fully grown, the scales on a female pinecone open. In late October, these winged seeds begin falling to the ground. The long wing helps the seed float away from the shade of its parent tree. The seed needs plenty of sunlight to grow.

Some female pinecones, such as those found on the jack pine and lodgepole pine trees, need heat to open. Forest fires create enough heat to open these pinecones and allow their seeds to fall out.

Most adult shortleaf pine trees are cut down for lumber when they are about 35 years old. It's hard to find a shortleaf pine tree that is more than 100 years old. However, a 314-year-old shortleaf pine was discovered in Arkansas not long ago.

The Cycle Begins Again

After a long winter, pine tree seeds sprout in spring. In time, they grow into tall adult trees. These mighty pines provide homes for animals. Their long green branches give shade to hikers and campers on sunny days. During its life cycle, the shortleaf pine tree makes our world a more beautiful place to live!

Life Cycle of a Shortleaf Pine Tree

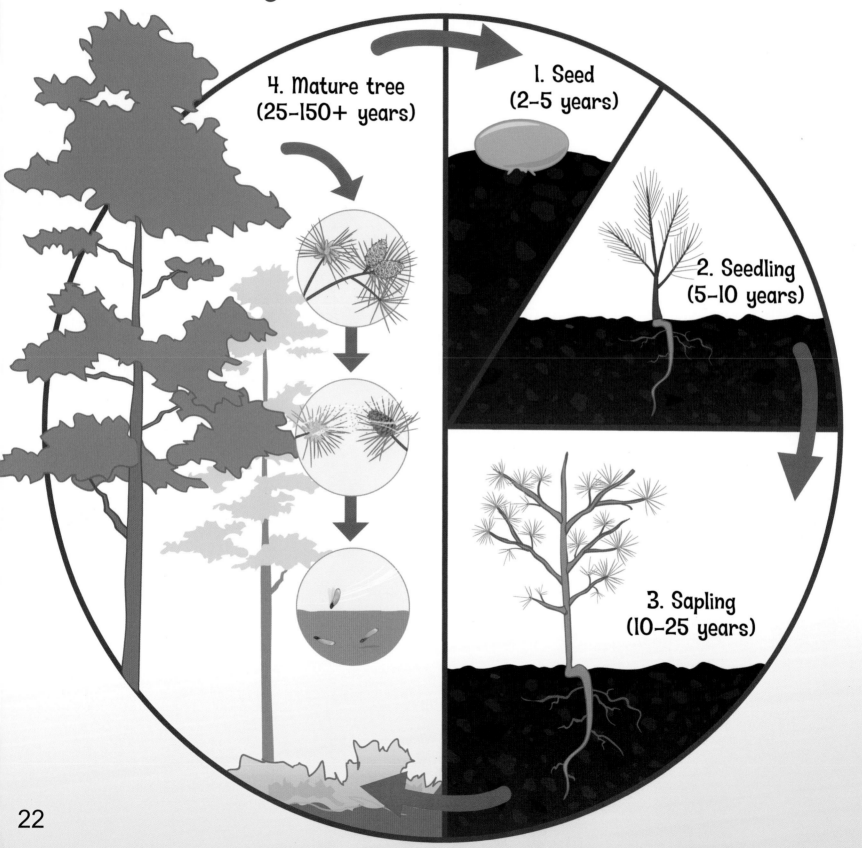

4. Mature tree
(25-150+ years)

1. Seed
(2-5 years)

2. Seedling
(5-10 years)

3. Sapling
(10-25 years)

Fun Facts

- One of the tallest pine trees in the world, named Boogerman Pine, is still growing in the Great Smoky Mountains National Park. This white pine stands 186 feet (57 m) tall!

- Certain pine trees are endangered in some states. This means the trees are in danger of dying out, or no longer existing. The shortleaf pine is an endangered tree in Illinois.

- Some farms grow pine trees that will become beautiful Christmas trees. In the United States, 500,000 acres (200,000 hectares) of farmland are used to grow Christmas trees.

- The longest pinecone in the world grows on the sugar pine tree. Some of these large female pinecones are up to 21 inches (53 cm) long! Sugar pine trees grow in the mountainous areas of the western United States.

Shortleaf pine forest

Glossary

fertilizes—joins male plant parts with female plant parts to make seeds

germination—when a seed begins to grow into a new plant

lumber—boards cut from logs

mature—having reached full growth or development

nutrients—parts of food that are used for growth

photosynthesis—a process plants use to make food and oxygen

pollen—a powder made by flowers to help them create new seeds

roots—the part of a plant that grows underground and soaks up water and nutrients

sapling—a young tree that is taller than 6.6 feet (2 m) and has a trunk that is less than 4 inches (10 cm) around

scales—the thin, overlapping leaves on the pinecones of some evergreens

seed—the part of a flower that will grow into a new plant

seedling—a young tree that is about 6 to 80 inches (15 to 200 cm) tall and has a trunk that is less than 4 inches (10 cm) around

To Learn More

More Books to Read

Cooper, Jason. *Pine Tree*. Vero Beach, Fla.: Rourke Pub., 2004.

Godwin, Sam. *From Little Acorns: A First Look at the Life Cycle of a Tree*. Minneapolis: Picture Window Books, 2005.

Kalman, Bobbie, and Kathryn Smithyman. *The Life Cycle of a Tree*. New York: Crabtree Pub. Co., 2002.

Tagliaferro, Linda. *The Life Cycle of a Pine Tree*. Mankato, Minn.: Capstone Press, 2007.

On the Web

FactHound offers a safe, fun way to find educator-approved Internet sites related to this book.

Here's what you do:
1. Visit *www.facthound.com*
2. Choose your grade level.
3. Begin your search.

This book's ID number is 9781404851627

Look for all of the books in the Amazing Science: Life Cycles series:

From Caterpillar to Butterfly: Following the Life Cycle
From Egg to Snake: Following the Life Cycle
From Mealworm to Beetle: Following the Life Cycle
From Pup to Rat: Following the Life Cycle
From Puppy to Dog: Following the Life Cycle
From Seed to Apple Tree: Following the Life Cycle
From Seed to Daisy: Following the Life Cycle
From Seed to Maple Tree: Following the Life Cycle
From Seed to Pine Tree: Following the Life Cycle
From Tadpole to Frog: Following the Life Cycle